TENANT'S REVENGE

TENANT'S REVENGE

HOW TO TAME YOUR LANDLORD

BY ANDY KANE

ILLUSTRATIONS BY STEVE SOEFFING

PALADIN PRESS
BOULDER, COLORADO

Also by Andy Kane:

. . . And This Is the Bathroom:

How to Really Sell Real Estate

Care and Feeding of Tenants

How to Avoid a Sexual Harassment Suit:

and what to do if you can't

Tenant's Revenge: How to Tame Your Landlord
by Andy Kane

Copyright © 1983 by Andy Kane

ISBN 0-87364-258-9
Printed in the United States of America

Published by Paladin Press, a division of
Paladin Enterprises, Inc., P.O. Box 1307,
Boulder, Colorado 80306, USA.
(303) 443-7250

Direct inquires and/or orders to the above address.

Visit our Web site at www.paladin-press.com

CONTENTS

PREFACE

After the success of my book *Care and Feeding of Tenants* (Paladin Press, 1982), a landlord's guide to handling tenants, many people mentioned that I had seriously shifted the balance of power in the landlord's favor. Talk show and newspaper interviewers pointed out that with this valuable information now wholly in the hands of the landlord, he could, in effect, wage war on his tenants using nuclear arms, and they would still be using crossbows.

I can't say that I am sorry, because that is exactly the way I intended it to be. I do, however, have a soft spot in my heart (a very small one) for the underdog. So at the urging of my son, tenants, wife, publisher, and assorted do-gooder groups, I have decided to give equal time to the plight of the tenant. Thus came about *Tenant's Revenge, How to Tame Your Landlord*.

By writing this book to help tenants survive the rental process, I will benefit greatly. First, my conscience will be eased. And my wallet will be fatter so I will be able to drink a little more and work a little less. But most importantly, when I go to meet that big landlord in the sky, the ledger book will list some good under my name for helping the unfortunate tenants of the world.

Although I have never been a tenant, I have dealt with tenants since the age of nine and by relating some of the tactics that tenants successfully used against me, there is a chance that I may brighten some tenant's day. Please keep in mind that the landlord, in his infinite wisdom, is usually right, so the procedures in this book should be used only in that one-in-a-million case when the landlord may make a small error.

I would never suggest breaking any law, so please consider the end result before you undertake any scheme that may not be within the law. The government is a very poor landlord in the subsidized housing projects it operates in the United States, and it is an even worse landlord of the jails. You will find the accommodations drafty, overcrowded, noisy, and the food less than gourmet. Keep the consequences of breaking the law in mind at all times in dealing with your landlord.

It is said that the first automobile race began when the second auto was built. The same is true of tenant/landlord problems. They began when the first tenant rented the first cave. The tenant probably didn't like the color of the walls, or the moss on the floor needed shampooing, or the stalactites were dripping, or the guy in the next cave had loud parties and played his drums until all hours. The problems have continued throughout civilized history. Landlords had certain remedies for tenant problems in the old days that are no longer available to them today. Boiling in oil and beheading are no longer approved methods of quieting a dissatisfied tenant, although I think a lot of problems could be resolved if these solutions were brought back today. The courts and justice system are actually protective of the tenant, and the deck is stacked against the landlord.

I believe that the landlord should provide exactly the services he agreed to and that the tenant should pay exactly the rent he agreed to pay. That's a very simple agreement. It's just fair play. But when the tenant or landlord does not live up to his part of the agreement, the trouble begins. If you are not paying your rent, you are the guilty party—*don't blame the landlord*. If the landlord is not providing the services he agreed to provide, it is he who is the guilty party.

Usually the big problem is deciding which party is telling the truth. Many tenants are better liars than are landlords because they have had more experience at it. Practice makes perfect.

I would suggest trying to get along with your landlord, and if all else fails, you always have *Tenant's Revenge, How to Tame Your Landlord* to fall back on.

It is a good country that allows freedom of speech, and I am sure that if this book were written in some other country, there is very little chance that it would ever get on the book shelves. In this country, you can complain and possibly be heard and effect changes. We are indeed fortunate to live in the U.S.A. God bless America!

1. ANATOMY OF A LANDLORD

If you are aware of the landlord's makeup, your dealings with him may be easier. One thing you should always keep in mind is that your landlord is (or should be) a businessman. His goal should be to realize a profit. Each and every month after the bills are paid, there should be something left over for his profit. Some landlords are satisfied with a small profit, some like a little more. Let's look at the constitution of a typical landlord, starting at the top.

Hat—A black top hat is fine. Gives the professional appearance. Usually has a steel liner to protect skull from bricks and flower pots being dropped off roof by tenants.

Brain—Well-developed. Works like a Japanese computer and voice-stress analyzer. Immediately separates fact from fiction when listening to tenants' complaints and excuses.

Face—Always appears friendly, honorable, trustworthy, clean, brave, and reverent. When the rent is due, his eyes are capable of seeing tenants hiding behind closed doors.

Hair—Clean, close-cropped. This prevents tenants'

roaches from nesting in hair and traveling home with the landlord.

Shoulders—Wide, strong. These support the weight of providing tender, loving care to hundreds of tenants, without regard to personal safety.

Arms and Hands—Muscular arms and calloused knuckles from knocking loudly on doors. Left hand closes like a steel trap as soon as money is inserted in palm. Right hand has lightning-fast reaction. Can handle small weapon like a Green Beret.

Vest—Dark, respectable color over bullet-proof material. Has secret pockets for cash.

Heart—This item is not part of landlord's makeup. In its place, you will find a calculator.

Stomach—Sometimes called guts. Usually made of cast iron to withstand aroma of tenants' quarters.

Belt—Thick to hold large ring of assorted keys similar to those used by jailers. Shows evidence of being taken in a bit because inflation has eaten up landlord's profit.

Trousers—Custom-made. One pocket has time lock and audible alarm. Neatly tailored to conceal small weapon. Reinforced from knees down and in seat to protect from dog bites.

Legs—Extremely well-developed from climbing tenement stairs and kicking kids, dogs, and cats. Able to spring landlord over puddles between sidewalk and his Rolls Royce in a single bound.

Shoes—Usually hand-tooled, pointed leather boots. Protects feet against rat bites. Pointed boots are also excellent for motivating tenant who is lax about paying rent.

Courage—This is not visible, but you can be sure it is there. Landlords have no fear and will tread where even the police fear to go. Going to the moon would be no

problem for our landlord. At least as he took the "one great step for mankind," he would not have to worry about encountering a junkie with a switchblade.

Your landlord is a breed unto himself. He has the makeup of the pilgrim, explorer, soldier of fortune, bounty hunter, and entrepreneur rolled into one.

If you are going to best him in a duel of wits, you should lay your ground work well. Since he is basically interested in making money, you will not have problems if you always pay your rent on time. Money is the sole motivation of the landlord. If you are out to hurt him or get revenge, forget about physical harm and concentrate on taking his money. You can take his money either by not paying rent, or by malicious acts, such as leaving all the windows open while the furnace is operating.

If you force the landlord to use some of the money he has buried in his backyard, it will be good for our economy. Getting this money back in circulation is good for the country. You are demonstrating your patriotism and are a good American. God bless America!

2. FINDING YOUR CASTLE

Obviously you are out to get a roof over your head. How big a roof depends on the number of brats you have in your family. Basic shelter is one of mankind's principal needs. You have probably heard of people in India living in doorways, people in Africa living in thatched huts, others living on boats because there was no room on land, some living in caves, and even in the rural South today, families calling an abandoned school bus home. There are landlords around who will rent you any type of hovel you are willing to live in.

You may be satisfied with meager accommodations such as these. Some of my tenants would be happy living in a discarded refrigerator. Some would even be satisfied living in the cardbord refrigerator *box*. But then again, once in a long while I find a tenant who wants something just a little bit better than the ordinary.

Before you set out to find the apartment of your dreams, set some guidelines based on your personal needs. Consider your requirements carefully. Write them down to be sure you have taken everything into consideration. Let me outline some possibilities.

Apartment Over a Bar

If you drink a lot and like noise and the smell of smoke and stale beer, try an apartment over a bar. You will be where the action is. You will not have to drive after drinking, and if you get behind in the rent, there is always a chance you can work some rent off cleaning up, restocking the cooler, or tending bar. The same applies to pizza-freaks or amusement-nuts. Find an apartment over one of these businesses, and you will probably have reduced rent due to the nature of the business. Not everyone will live over a noisy, late-night establishment, so vacancies are hard to fill. Many apartments are large and can accommodate families with kids and pets. You can save money and enjoy your favorite pastime.

Slums

Older, dilapidated buildings (sometimes called slums) provide comfortable accommodations for many down-and-outers, large families, and minorities. If you don't need fancy, elaborate accommodations, why pay for them? You will usually have to fight off six other crazy tenants for the good apartments. The slum will be easy to obtain, and since supply and demand dictates rents, it will probably be cheaper. Every city has a cheap section. You have to look for it, but somewhere it will be there waiting with open arms for you and your clan.

Private Homes Converted to Apartments

There are many private homes that, because of the high cost of taxes and energy, are no longer practical for single-family use. Some have been converted to sleeping rooms with a common kitchen, and some have been converted to two-, three-, or four-family use. These converted homes will usually rent for less than new complexes, since often they are paid for and owned by individuals instead of corporations bent on making a big profit to keep their shareholders happy. You will find these rooms in the residential sections of most cities. They provide economical accommodations for many tenants. Usually there is no credit or reference check and only the first month's rent and a security deposit is required. You will probably deal directly with the landlord, and he may be a part-time or mom-and-pop operation.

Duplexes, Double Houses, Older Apartment Buildings

Most of these are owned by individuals, some of whom may actually reside in the property and rent the apartments themselves. This means you are again dealing with amateur or part-time landlords. If you have some skeletons in your closet, your best bet is this type of landlord. You can usually pull the wool over their eyes with ease. They will probably not be experienced at evaluating tenants and will take you at face value. Many of these apartments are well maintained, since the landlord may reside in the property. There are many of these units in older cities, and they provide adequate shelter for your bucks.

Complexes, Condos, Townhouses

If you are looking for class, prestige, and high prices, these will fill the bill. You may have pools, saunas, bikini-clad chicks, doormen, security, and other assorted frills. Most complexes of this type are well maintained since the tenants may refuse to pay the exorbitant rents if they are not.

Deciding just what type of accommodations you are looking for before you begin your search will save you and hopeful landlords lots of time and trouble. Be realistic. Even if your grimy brats rarely play with matches in the closet and your Great Dane graduated from obedience school with top honors, a fancy, singles' complex is not the place for you.

Now that you've decided on a place you want to live, what makes you think that the landlord is going to choose *you* to be his tenant? Even in a depressed economy, he may not be *that* hard up. So before you make your first contact with the landlord, take stock of the impression you will be giving. You may be able to spruce yourself up—even if only for the hour it takes to get him to offer you a lease.

Put Your Best Foot Forward

When you approach a landlord to inspect the hovel of your dreams, you should make a good impression. The landlord gets his first impression as soon as you arrive. If you get out of a bus carrying all your worldly possessions in a shopping bag and wearing tattered clothes, he may seriously doubt your ability to come up with the bread for next month's rent.

You should arrive in style. If you have a car, be sure it is clean. If you don't have one, borrow (or steal) one. If you have kids, leave them home. Make it appear that you can easily afford the joint. Get most of your money in dollar bills. Fold your wad with twenties and fifties on the outside. Then when you make the deposit, peel off the money, being sure the landlord sees the roll. Dress in your finest, unless you are a pimp, then dress down. Leave the mink and super-fly hat at home. Appear to be a good, law-abiding, clean-cut, all-American boy or girl.

If you have six rotten, screaming brats, leave five home. If the landlord asks how many kids you have, say "I have only one with me." This will create the impression that the others are grown, married, or living with your ex-husband. The gypsies are experts at this. One pulls up nicely dressed in a shiny Cadillac. Around the corner await five pick-up trucks loaded with kids, chickens, and distant relatives.

I have had the gypsy trick pulled on me. I rented to the Tom Williams family thinking it was a husband, wife, and two little ones. The next day I discovered the Williams family consisted of sixty-four people! Luckily I was able to get them out, but they put a gypsy curse on me, and I've had a bald spot on the top of my head ever since.

The same technique used with children is used with pets. If you don't bring your German shepherd, you may not be asked about pets. I had a friend who named his two-hundred-pound Great Dane Kitty. When a landlord would ask if he had a pet, he would reply, "Just Kitty, and she is no trouble at all." Many times he got an apartment with the landlord thinking he had a little kitten.

Another friend had a cat. He always mentioned it when renting. Many landlords were later surprised when they met his cat. It was an eighty-pound ocelot. With pets, play it by ear. If the landlord stipulates *no pets!— period,* tell him you don't have a pet, then bring it with you later. If there is a surcharge for pets, let yours run around loose. When it's feeding time, put its dish in front of your neighbor's door. That way the landlord will think it belongs to him and add five dollars to his rent. Your neighbor can probably afford it better anyway.

Apartment Living May Be Hazardous to Your Health

Apartment living can be hazardous to your health. You may not find this warning printed on the side of a building as it is on a pack of cigarettes, but the danger is there. If 1 family in 100 is struck by fire each year, and you live in a complex with 100 families, you have a chance of being cremated while you sleep. I have noticed that many fires occur in apartment houses. If the property does not have a smoke detection system, get a smoke alarm for your own unit. At least you will have some warning when the drunk downstairs sets his bed on fire with a cigarette.

Crime also has a way of hitting apartment dwellers. Again, look at the statistics. They are always greater when you congregate a bunch of losers in one spot. Tenants, as a group, are convicted of crimes at a rate much higher than homeowners. A survey of the prisoners at Attica Prison when the bloody uprising was quelled by the New York state police indicated that 97 percent were tenants previous to being sentenced to prison. Common sense tells you that you are going to be very vulnerable living in a complex with hundreds of potential thieves, muggers, child molesters, and rapists. I would suggest that you be on your toes, keep your doors and windows locked, and use extreme caution around your complex. If possible, carry a weapon and be sure you know how to use it.

Apartments are havens for junkies. Keep your eyes open for addicts in and around your building. Calling the police or telling the landlord is a waste of time. They cannot do anything to stop crime in the area. Addicts will steal to support their habits. They will kill, they will do just about anything to get or stay high. By

Man in wheelchair mugged in high rise

Miller was robbed of his wallet as he pushed his wheelchair through the seventh-floor hallway at River Park Commons, 185 Mount Hope Ave., Monday night.

In the past six months, three burglaries and one other robbery at the tower have been investigated by city police, said Capt. Gordon Urlacher of Highland Section.

"When you consider that a high rise has more units than an average street, that's not many burglaries and robberies," he said.

There are about 200 apartments in the housing tower, formerly named Genesee Gateway Apartments. A mixture of low-income and elderly people live in the tower, and a small percentage of handicapped people also live there

Miller has tried to move elsewhere, but waiting lists exist at subsidized apartment towers that have access to the handicapped.

having a weapon and knowing how to use it, you will enhance your chances of staying alive until the rent is due again.

Many times arrests and other crime information appear in the newspaper, and the location is mentioned. Keep abreast of local news to find out what crime is going on in any complex you are considering resting your weary bones in.

If you inspect a property with the landlord and are considering renting it, you should leave, drive around the block, and return. The landlord will think you have gone. Go to an adjoining unit and knock on the door. Ask the tenant what he thinks of the building. Are there roaches and crime? Is there heat in winter? Does the landlord fix things? Ask anything else that may interest you.

Weigh the answers carefully. If this tenant is of a different color, religion, nationality, or has a personality conflict with you, he may lie to discourage you from renting. If you are a chick with a hell of a body, and he is a Don Juan, he may tell you the place is super to get you to move in next door. If you have reason to doubt the tenant, check more than one.

3. WHERE TO LIVE

Once you have decided what you are looking for, the next step is to decide where you want to live. Luckily, in this country you can choose to live just about anywhere. Unless you are on parole, in the federal witness protection program, or an Indian relegated to

the reservation, you can decide where you prefer to hang your dirty T-shirt and put your six-pack on ice.

Assuming that you and the other crummy creatures you call your family are acceptable to most landlords, you should be able to pick an area where you are comfortable. If you are employed, you may want to be close to your work to eliminate unnecessary commuting time and expense. If you are a wetback, displaced person, or non-English-speaking person, you would be wise to stay with your people. That is the path of least resistance, and you will be happiest there.

Persons of various ethnic groups have a much greater acceptance by landlords if they remain together in one area. If the landlord speaks English and you speak Spanish, there is a problem in communicating even the smallest problem or complaint. If you are in a Spanish area, there is bound to be someone who can act as interpreter. If you are in a predominantly English-speaking neighborhood and you don't speak English, you are going to have difficulties.

If you remember the tower of Babel story from the Bible, you know that very little got done after the workers began speaking different languages. Take a tip from the Bible and stay with your own kind. This is a cruel world and race is a factor that causes lots of concern for landlords.

Once you have decided what you are looking for and where you want it to be located, the next task is to find an apartment. This may be easy in some locations, and difficult or next to impossible in others. If it's easy, you're lucky. If it's hard, I may be able to help you out. The obvious approach is to look in the classifieds or for vacancy signs. Visit apartment complexes. If this is not productive, try some of these techniques.

Obituaries

Although your marriage license contains the clause "till death do us part," leases do not. The lease of a dead person is not terminated by his demise. And his estate may sublease the apartment to you. The undertaker, neighbors, or relatives will usually be able to tell you who the executor of the will is so you can contact that person.

Births

Check these out. Does the happy couple now have three rug-rats in a one-bedroom apartment? Or is it their first kid and the landlord does not allow kids? Many times this blessed event will cause a vacancy.

Knock on Doors

This is possibly one of the most productive ways to find an apartment. Don't ask just if they are considering moving, ask if they know of anyone in the area that may be moving.

Check with Agencies

Realtors and rental agencies are good places to look for vacancies. I own the largest rental agency in my city. Landlords list their vacancies with me because I charge the tenant a fee for my service. The landlord's theory is that my fee will discourage the scum, tramps, and deadbeats. The people who pay my fee will be a cut above the average tenant. Any bum can get a day-old paper out of the trash and call about the classifieds, but my clients plunk down cold, hard cash for my service.

When dealing with a rental service or realtors, apply in person. Many companies save vacancies for tenants that they can evaluate in person. They may tell you over the phone that no vacancies exist because they don't want to take a chance on encouraging an undesirable. Go in person and pay any fee that is required. It's well worth it.

Criminals

The daily paper contains many reports of persons arrested for rape, robbery, murder, and such. The arrested person's address is usually given in the news item. You may contact him at the jail and make arrangements to sublease his apartment. He can probably use the money to buy cigarettes for the next five years or a hacksaw blade.

Promotions

The financial section of the daily paper usually contains the promotions for the area—"Charlie Tenant of 48-A Open Arms Court has been promoted to chief widget washer at the Oakland plant of Wesley Widget Company. He will assume his duties starting next

month." Since he will be moving out of town, he will not need his pad at 48-A Open Arms Court. Go over right away, congratulate him, slap him on the back, and sublease his apartment.

4. LEASES AND MORE LEASES

Leases are designed to protect the landlord and be used against you, the tenant, at a future date, if you step out of line. There are basically two kinds of leases. First is the do-it-yourself, ten-cent, stationery-store-bought blank form, used by most part-time, mom-and-pop-type small landlords, who own a double, four-plex or old complex. This is the most common lease, and it is practically worthless.

The second is the lease type used by complexes and large landlords which may be four or five pages long and contain the "whereases" and the "therefores" the legal profession loves to use. It will tell you when you can use the pool, the penalty for peeing in it, what you can wear in it, and its average chlorine content. It will say when you can play your stereo and at what decibel level. It will contain all sorts of clauses and penalties for payment and nonpayment of rents. It will specify what type of pet is allowed and its weight—for example, a dog under twelve pounds. (I wonder if you could be evicted if your dog gained weight after you moved in!) There may be a charge for a child. (I also wonder if they would take the brat and let you stay if you didn't pay the kid charge.) The lease will tell you exactly where to

A Lease

Made and executed **Between** ANDY KANE
of the CITY of ROCHESTER , New York, of the first
part and DAVID SMITH, ISABELE SMITH

of the CITY of ROCHESTER , New York, of the second
part, this 3 RD day of DECEMBER in the year One thousand

nine hundred and EIGHTY ONE

In Consideration of the rents and covenants hereinafter expressed, the said party
of the first part has   Demised and Leased   and does hereby demise and lease to the
said party of the second part
the following premises, viz.: 561 E. BROAD ST. UPPER
APT, 1 GARAGE, TENANT IS TO PAY GAS, ELECTRIC
AND HEAT, SHOVEL WALK AND CUT GRASS

with the privileges and appurtenances, for and during the term of ONE YEAR
from the 1 ST day of JANUARY , 1982, which term will
end DEC 31 ST 1982

And the said part**ies** of the second part covenant that they will pay to the party
of the first part for the use of said premises the monthly rent of THREE HUNDRED
FIFTY 00/100 Dollars ($ 350.00), to be paid on 1 ST OF EACH
MONTH IN ADVANCE. TENANT ALSO WILL PAY $350
SECURITY DEPOSIT AND $350 FOR LAST MONTHS RENT

    And Provided Said part**ies** of the second part shall fail to pay said rent, or any
part thereof when it becomes due, OR WITHIN 5 DAYS
, it is agreed that the said party of the
first part may sue for the same, or re-enter said premises, or resort to any legal remedy.

    The party of the 1 ST part agree**s** to pay all CITY/COUNTY taxes to be
assessed on said premises during said term
~~TENANT SHALL PAY ALL WATER CHARGES~~ AK.

    The part**ies** of the second part covenant**s** that at the expiration of said term
they will surrender up said premises to the party of the first part in as good condition as now, necessary wear and damage by the elements excepted.
TENANT SHALL SUPPLY HIS OWN TRASH RECEPTICALS

      Witness the hands and seals of the said parties, the day and year first above
written

David Smith / Isabele Smith _____ [L. S.]

Andy Kane _____ [L. S.]

park and what size car is allowed. If you read it closely, you will probably find that it removes all the rights that were guaranteed by the Constitution. If you are not a wizard with words, or are incapable of reading between the lines, I suggest that you have an attorney read it over before you sign.

Stationery Store Leases

If you have had any problems in the past with landlords of big complexes, they have probably recorded the events for posterity (the court and credit bureau). You will be wise then to deal with small landlords who may not belong to the credit bureau. By small landlords, I do not mean landlords who are only five-foot tall, but landlords who own only a few units. These landlords will not have a lawyer on retainer and will try to avoid the expense of eviction and court appearances. Most of them are part-time landlords who hold a full-time job. If they must go to court, they lose time from their other job. They are the easiest to bamboozle or flimflam.

The stationery store lease will tell who the landlord is, who the tenant is, where the apartment is, and how much rent is due. It may contain clauses regarding who maintains what (trash, utilities, yard). This lease, whether typed or printed, is not carved in stone. It can be changed with the stroke of a pen if the landlord and tenant agree. If you don't like something, tell the landlord you would like to change it. You both should initial the change.

Read the lease carefully. Is five days enough time for you to get the rent in? Fifteen days would probably be better. Tell the landlord your check comes from the "home office" and sometimes does not arrive until the seventh of the month. Tell him you must have fifteen days to be safe. This way if your girl friend goes to jail

on the first of the month for prostitution, you can bail
her out, get her back on the street, and have her earn
enough money to pay the rent by the fifteenth.

If the lease contains a clause that does not allow
subleasing, try to have it stricken. If you ever disagree
with the landlord, you can retaliate by subleasing to a
tribe of Indians, boat people who have entered the
country illegally, or radical undesirables. If you really
want to make some easy money, you can do a multiple
sublease, which is guaranteed to give the landlord an
ulcer, heart failure, or a nervous breakdown.

The Multiple Sublease, Lease, Lease . . .

Go to a stationery store and make ten copies of
your lease. Also have ten keys made. On the back of
each lease, type the following:

I, Joe Tenant, do hereby assign

my lease to,

    ___A. SUCKER___

for the remainder of its term.

My security deposit and last

month's rent have been paid to

me by the new tenant.

Date 6-15-82

Tenant JOE TENANT

At least thirty days before you are going to move, place an ad in the paper to sublease your apartment. Make an appointment with each one who calls to see it. The appointments should be about forty-five minutes apart so the potential tenants don't meet. Sign the sublease with each one, get your security deposit and last month's rent, and give each a shiny new key. Tell each one that he can move in on the first.

After you have successfully collected ten security deposits and ten last month's rents, I suggest that you move immediately. The farther you get from this apartment, the better it will be. Argentina has a nice climate! The take should be four or five grand, so you should be able to afford good accommodations. Can you imagine your landlord's problem when ten moving trucks and ten tenants arrive on the first of the month, all with leases and keys for the same apartment?

The Complex Lease

Complexes are usually owned by smart investors, corporations, or conglomerates. These tycoons don't

stay in business by being stupid. They have perfected their leases by trial and error. The leases have been drawn up by their attorneys, who have put all their knowledge into taking advantage of the tenant and reaping the most profit for the corporation. Almost anything that happens, including nuclear attacks, will be covered. If you are not good as gold, clean as a whistle, and a steady church-goer, you will probably not get the apartment unless there is an overabundance of available units in the area.

The complex-owners do their best to avoid problems. Their leases are not subject to change and usually their managers or superintendents do not have the power to make any alterations in the printed forms. Once you sign, rest assured that you will pay, unless you disappear and your wages cannot be garnisheed. If you have every intention of paying and you are sure you can live up to the specifications set forth in the lease, go ahead and enjoy yourself.

Some Good Points

Complexes often cater to a certain clientele. Many are for the elderly. They have really wild bingo games, trips to the Lawrence Welk Show and a lot of ladies with blue hair. There is a complex on the West Coast which caters to nudists. You can save on dry cleaning if you are into this fad. There are complexes which attract singles only. If you are a single or a divorcee, you might be very happy there. Look them all over and get what you pay for. Be sure you fit in, and you will probably survive the full term of the lease.

If you are seriously considering moving to a complex, find out if any tenants are subleasing their units before you sign a lease with the management. Since rents escalate regularly due to inflation, you will save

money if you can take over an existing lease. Be sure you don't get involved in a multiple sublease situation. If the guy looks like he is about to disappear and leave ten leases and keys floating about, give him a small deposit to hold until the first of the month.

If there is the possibility of getting an apartment without a lease, you may avoid problems in the future. Leases are restrictive. If you have an idea that your job may not be steady, or that you may have to duck out to avoid paying child support or stay clear of an ex-wife, you would be better off in a month-to-month rental.

5. BREAKING A LEASE

A lease is written to protect the landlord from tenants. It usually spells out the duties of landlord and tenant, but if you notice, it says mostly what the tenant must do to remain a tenant and what penalty the tenant will suffer if he disobeys the master—usually the loss of his security deposit and/or eviction. Most landlords develop and perfect their leases after various experiences with previous tenants.

Before you begin a complicated campaign to get out of your lease, try one simple method. Ask the landlord to let you out of your lease. There is a good chance he may have been in your apartment for six months of a twenty-four-month lease. There are eighteen months remaining at that fixed rent. If inflation has increased rents for the type of apartment you are living in by 10 percent, the landlord will lose money if you stay the full term. He may be happy to see you go so he can rerent at the current, higher rate. Give it a try. You have nothing to lose. If you are not successful, then you can try a trick or two.

The Noisy Neighbor

All leases entitle the tenant to quiet enjoyment of the surroundings. Even if your building is quiet, you can create the impression that the building is full of tenants who are running amuck and disturbing the peace. About 3 A.M. some quiet morning, call the police and report that the tenant in 3-B is playing his stereo full blast, drunk, and fighting with his wife. Go out and place several broken beer bottles in the hall near his door. Open your window enough to put your radio in it and turn out your lights. When you see the cops pull into the parking lot, crank your radio on full blast and be sure it is turned to the local boog-a-loo station. When you hear the cops at the neighbor's apartment door, shut your radio off. They will assume the noise was coming from your neighbor's apartment. They will make a report of this occurrence. Do the same thing for the next three nights. Then go down to the police department and obtain copies of the police reports indicating that your neighbor was disturbing the peace.

Confront the landlord with the charge that he has allowed the place to go to the dogs. You can't get any sleep. Threaten to call in the media and show them the reports if he does not let you break the lease. There is a good chance he will do it to avoid bad publicity.

The Dead Tenant

You have found a nice apartment across town. You know from past experience that your landlord will not be easy to deal with. Drop the word to several of your neighbors and the landlord, if possible, that you are heading out about the twenty-eighth of the month to see your aunt (boy friend, girl friend, or war buddy) in St. Louis. About the thirtieth, have a friend go over and

tell the landlord that you were killed in a traffic accident on Route 5 in Kalamazoo. Have your friend tell
him that she is going to clean out the apartment right
away, so he can rerent it and not lose any rent. "Joe
Tenant would have wanted it that way, God rest his
soul," she should cluck, wiping her eyes. She should ask
him to please make out a check to the Estate of Joe
Tenant so it can be forwarded for funeral expenses.

If he does not go along with that, have a friend call
and say that he is Alphonse Bell, attorney for the Estate
of Joe Tenant. Have the attorney ask for the security
deposit check, so it can be used for funeral expenses. If
the landlord does not knuckle under, have your attorney threaten to call the local papers and tell them of the
landlord who is withholding burial money for an accident victim. I'm sure you will succeed in breaking the
lease and getting your security deposit back.

Your "Father" Must Move In

You want out of the lease, but you know that your
landlord has not allowed tenants to get out of their
leases in the past. So go to skid row, a public park, or a
sleazy dive, and adopt a "father." He should be attired
in a five-year-old, baggy, dirty, wrinkled suit—preferably
one reeking of urine and decorated with a little vomit.
Explain that you are trying to get out of a lease and
would like to hire him for a few minutes. A bottle of
wine or five bucks is adequate payment. Take him to
your building and tell your landlord that your father has
been evicted from his apartment and will be moving in
with you because he can't keep a job due to his alcohol
problem. Mention that you would much rather seek
other, larger accommodations but that your lease has
six months remaining. Any landlord with a brain in his

head will be happy to see you leave rather than bring
this human garbage to his complex.

Changed Your Mind

Many times you fall in love with an apartment and
place a deposit on it only to learn later that day of one
twice as good for less money. If you go back and ask for
your deposit, you will get only a horselaugh. The landlord will keep the bucks and the law is on his side. You
took that apartment off the market, he turned away hundreds of potential tenants, he will lose rent, and so on.

If there was no mention of number of occupants, return with your "father" and ask if it is possible for him
to see it, since he will be living with you. If a father
figure is not available, try a gang of bikers. Every area
has a bikers' bar where you can recruit some help. Tell

them you are trying to convince a landlord, and they may even volunteer their services. If you use bikers, have them mention to the landlord that they will be having a "house warming party" as soon as they move in, and he is invited. He doesn't have to bring any booze, drugs, or broads because they will have plenty! If your landlord was smart enough to limit the number of tenants per unit, check for a pets clause.

Were pets allowed when you agreed to rent? If they were, return for one more look with your pets. Try to find two of the meanest mutts for your visit, preferably big German shepherds or Doberman Pinchers. Turn them loose as soon as you are out of the car so they can get dirty and jump on other tenants. When they knock an old lady down or bite a kid, say "He's just playing. Isn't that cute?"

The landlord will immediately mention that the painters have gone on strike, and your apartment may not be ready on the first. He will tell you how sorry he is and that the only fair thing would be to return your deposit.

Transferred Employee

Have a co-worker (if you work) call your landlord and say he is president of Silver Sledgehammer Watch Company and you are being transferred. If the landlord is so kind as to allow you to terminate your lease, future executives transferring into the area will be made aware of his cooperation and his units will be highly recommended. Try to get a co-worker who has more than a third-grade education to make the call, so the pitch will sound authentic.

6. REDECORATING ACCIDENTALLY

Landlords, being on a fixed renovation and repair budget, may from time to time lack funds for redecorating. You have requested, but did not receive, redecoration of your apartment. You have been a good tenant, paying rent on time and respecting the property, but the landlord refuses to consider your request. What alternatives are available?

The first and most commonly used remedy is simply to move to another apartment which you find more to your liking. If this is convenient, by all means I recommend you do this. You will probably be very happy in your new abode.

But you have a second alternative. Try to visualize this scene. You have definite reasons for preferring this apartment to all others. Maybe you are close to work, your girl friend, your mother-in-law, or you speak Swahili, and this is the only neighborhood where Swahili is spoken. You could pay for redecorating, but knowing the nature and habits of most tenants, I doubt that you will. Here is what some of my tenants did to redecorate.

They were in the kitchen cooking fried chicken in a pot of grease. Mysteriously, some of the grease boiled

33

over and presto—a small fire began which caused considerable smoke damage to the kitchen and required that the apartment be redecorated.

I would never recommend arson, but then again, accidents do happen. Your landlord will not complain because he has insurance and that will pay for the redecorating. If you are planning an accident, let me point out a few items.

First, consider the morality of an accident. You buy cigarettes and matches every day. You pay for them, they are yours, you take them home, and you light them up. No problem. People do it all the time. The only difference is that this time you buy a chicken. You pay for it, it's yours. What you do with your own property is your business. Instead of smoking a cigarette, you smoke a chicken! No problem. But be sure you prepare for your coming redecoration by working out a few details in advance.

Renter's Insurance

You should have renter's insurance. The landlord's insurance *does not* cover replacement of your personal possessions. It only covers his interest in the property. You should also take photos of all your possessions in the apartment and keep them in a safe place. *Do not keep them at home!* A good place is a safety deposit box or at your office. This will enable you to recall any item damaged or lost in any accident. Don't forget to take a photo of the contents of the clothes closet with all your designer jeans, expensive suits, and matched luggage. If you don't have items like these, try borrowing some from a prosperous friend.

Liability

Accidents are safer if the rest of the building is un-

occupied. A late-night fire could result in some panic and/or other tenants jumping out upper floor windows.

A Timely Vacation

An accident may make your apartment unliveable, so a good time for an accident is just as you are about to leave for a two-week vacation. If that is not convenient, your landlord will probably have to put you up in one of your area's fine, flea-bag hotels. In anticipation of an accident, you should have a bag packed and in your car. That way you will have some duds that won't make you smell like a hickory-smoked ham.

If you expect an accident in a week or two, don't take your dry cleaning or wash to be cleaned. Leave it in the closet with the door open. After the accident, the insurance company will pay to have all your clothing, drapes, and other items cleaned.

Other Benefits

In many areas, free help is available for victims of fires. The Red Cross, welfare, and The Volunteers of America have various programs which will provide cash and other assistance. Go see them and take advantage of their generosity. They will check with the fire department to verify that the fire did occur and then give you their assistance. You may get cash, furniture, or free meals.

All-in-all, accidents are not that bad. The landlord has a nice, fresh apartment at no expense to him. You have your new color scheme, the dry cleaner gets some work, the insurance adjuster stays busy, the firemen get a chance to play with their little red truck, the painter gets a couple of days' pay, and the economy of our country is stimulated. What a wonderful country we live in! God bless America!

7. YOUR DAY IN COURT

Sooner or later you and your landlord will test our judicial system in a court designed to handle tenant/landlord complaints. It may be called housing court, small claims court, or some other name, but they all work basically the same way. I'll take it step by step so that when the occasion arises, you will be familiar with the events.

The Subpoenas

Subpoenas will usually be served on you by certified mail requiring your signature, by a process server who must hand it to you personally, or if these methods fail, it may be published in a local paper. If you are using delaying tactics, you can buy some time by not signing for the letter and not admitting to the process server your true identity. You may confuse the issue even more by telling the process server that you are the new tenant, and the tenant he wants moved yesterday. Most process servers will not know you, so when one raps at the door and asks if you are so and so, deny it.

Preparation

Eventually you will be served and must face the judge. The subpoena will tell you who is suing you, for

Mailing No. **503983**

CITY COURT, CITY OF ROCHESTER
Civil Branch, Small Claims, Room One, Hall of Justice, Civic Center Plaza
Rochester, New York 14614

TO: Barb Perrault

1934 East Main St.

Rochester, NY 14609

TAKE NOTICE that   Andy Kane, Landlord, 1934 East Main St.

asks judgment in this Court against you for $220.00   , together with costs, upon the following claim: That on or about   Oct. 16,   , 19 81, or between   , 19 __ and   , 19____ , the plaintiff   occupied 1934 East Main St. and did not pay rent for same (by) XXXXX the defendant.

Wherefore, the plaintiff demands judgment against the defendant for the sum of $ 220.00 ± costs, together with costs and disbursements. $7.10

Andy Kane   1944 East Main St., Rochester, NY

There will be a hearing before the Court upon this claim on   Dec. 9,
_____, 19 81, at XXXXXXX
(1:30 P.M.) in the XXXXXXX (afternoon), in the City of Rochester, N.Y.
Part I, Hall of Justice, Civic Center Plaza.

You must appear and present your defense and any counterclaim you may desire to assert at the hearing at the time and place above set forth (a corporation must be represented by an attorney).   IF YOU DO NOT APPEAR, JUDGMENT WILL BE ENTERED AGAINST YOU BY DEFAULT EVEN THOUGH YOU MAY HAVE A VALID DEFENSE. If your defense or counterclaim, if any, is supported by witnesses, account books, receipts or other documents, you must produce them at the hearing. The Clerk, if requested, will issue subpoenas for witnesses, without fee therefore.

If you admit the claim, but desire time to pay, you must appear personally on the day set for the hearing, state to the Court that you desire time to pay and show your reasons for same.

NOTE: If you desire a jury trial, you must, before the day upon which you have been notified to appear, file with the Clerk of the Court a written demand for a trial by jury. You must also pay to the Clerk a jury fee of $15.00 and file an undertaking in the sum of $50.00 or deposit such sum in cash to secure the payment of any costs that may be awarded against you. You will also be required to make an affidavit specifying the issues of fact which you desire to have tried by a jury, stating that such trial is desired and demanded in good faith. Under the law, the Court may award $25.00 additional costs to the plaintiff if a jury trial is demanded by you and a decision is rendered against you.

Dated this   2   day of
Nov   19 81   _Evelyn Mance_
                                          Assistant Clerk

how much, for what reason, and when and where to
appear. Several things will influence the man in the
black bathrobe. You must prepare to put your best foot
forward. Collect any documents that may be in your
favor, such as:

- Police reports of noisy neighbors or violence in
  the building
- Rent receipts if they are favorable to your case
- Lists of violations of the fire and building codes
  obtained from the local building bureau
- Witnesses on your behalf
- Photo of dead rat in your kitchen or baby's bed-
  room. Photo is even more impressive if the rat is
  in baby's crib or if baby is holding it by the tail.
  If you can't find a rat in the basement or a neighbor's house, try the city dump. Be careful when

picking up dead rats. Sometimes they are only sleeping.

Our justice system is based on who can tell the best and most convincing lies in court. You should prepare your witnesses in advance to tell only what is beneficial to your case. Encourage them to embellish their stories. Tell them the judge will only believe half of what they say, so tell it twice as strong. That way, after the judge has diluted it in his mind, it will still carry some weight.

One last item—last, but probably most important— the day before you are to appear, have a female friend call the landlord late in the day. She should say, "This is small claims court calling about your case tomorrow. Due to the heavy case load, the calendar for tomorrow has been postponed for two weeks. Please appear at the same time two weeks from tomorrow." If your friend has done a good job, the landlord will not appear and you will win by default. Default is the best way to win. It takes the least amount of time, and it looks good that you appeared but the landlord did not.

Your Day in Court

The scales of justice are easily tipped in your favor. If you have laid the ground work as I have indicated, you will probably win. If the landlord took your call seriously and sayed home, you have already won!

First let's decide what your defense will be in case he does show up. *You paid the rent* (whether you did or not). Show all your past rent receipts and tell how you have paid your rent every month, but last month, the landlord took the rent and said he would mail you a receipt because he forgot his receipt book. Your brother-in-law (witness) was there and saw it all. Your landlord will not be able to produce a witness who saw

you *not* pay. You have an excellent chance of tipping the scales in your favor.

You are *not paying your rent because*—lay out your reasons. Show the violations from the fire department and the building bureau and a photo of a dead rat (or even better, bring it in a plastic bag). Sob that the landlord has refused to do anything about the problems . . . all he does is take the rent. Play on the judge's sympathy. Maybe bring one of your brats with a bandage on his finger where the rat bit him while he was sleeping. Don't take the bandage off in court to show the landlord or judge because the wound may get infected and you already have enough problems. Tell the judge how you used the rent to buy rat and roach bait to rid the property of the infestation. Show respect to the judge and dress neatly.

Don't shout or yell. Have your girl friend (witness) tell how the house is so cold in the winter that you can see your breath, the water in the toilet has a film of ice over it, and the kids have walking pneumonia. You are doing your best to find other accommodations, but things are tough. Give him a date (about thirty days away) and tell him you are sure you will find something by then. The judge will probably believe you and decide in your favor, plus give you another thirty days free rent. The scales will tip in your favor. This is a good country. God bless America!

8. FREE RENT

All greedy tenants perk up when they hear the phrase "free rent." In fact, some will go nuts for free anything. There are several ways to get free or reduced rent. For some reason, when the Lord created the earth he made, in addition to man and woman, tenants and landlords. I think being a tenant or a landlord is somehow determined by genes or chromosomes or something like that, and you have been cast as a tenant. Most tenants like to live as cheaply as possible, so that other funds may be diverted to booze, dope, women, or horses. That's understandable.

Welfare

One of the most popular methods of getting free rent in this wonderful country is to go on welfare, sometimes called the dole, public assistance, or the gravy train. It may cause you some embarrassment, but then again, it may be worth it. When you make the application, borrow two or three of your sister's kids and drag them along. Most allotments are based on family size, so the more the merrier. Leave your husband (if you own one) at home. They will usually give you more if there

43

is no breadwinner in the family. Tell them you don't know where the bum is.

When you have been accepted, immediately request more money for clothing for the kids. Check and see if there is a "welfare rights" organization in your area. Seek them out and join. They are experts at getting all they can get for nothing.

Subsidized Housing

In the past few years, Uncle Sam has developed many plans to assist people in obtaining decent shelter. Some programs help the landlord obtain low interest loans or bonds so he can rent his property at a lower-than-market value. Some pay the costs of operating a building. Some give direct aid to the tenant. They are all paid for by tax dollars.

If you are considering applying for this type of subsidized housing, call and get the guidelines for income levels that are eligible. Once you find that out, you may have to rearrange your finances to fit the mold and qualify. Many will have a formula saying you must have less than a certain amount in the bank, must not own a car, and must make less than a certain amount per year. You should then open a second account at another bank using your initials or an alias instead of your name. Register your car in your brother-in-law's name. Tell your boss that if he doesn't give you a verification of wages for less than you earn, you are going to start a fire in the wood shop or pour oil on the stairs to cause accidents. If you have done your homework correctly, your application should go through without a hitch. Don't park your Cadillac in the tenant's lot. Leave it around the corner.

Work

Many tenants may not know what this word means,

so I will explain it. It means to perform or carry out a task, exert yourself in labor, fulfill duties, to toil, and so on. In general, it means that if you get off your keester and do something of value, you will be rewarded. The reward may be a pat on the head, cold, hard cash, or *free rent*.

Many things need doing around an apartment house, and since you are there as a tenant, you are in a good position to do these things. Grass needs cutting, apartments need cleaning and showing, snow needs shoveling, the building needs painting and minor repairs—all these can be accomplished, for which the landlord may give you credit towards your rent. This is also known as bartering. It is one thing the IRS hates because there is usually no record made of this and taxes are not paid. It works well for both parties and you can use the money you save to live a little better.

House Sitting

Just like baby sitting, you can watch someone's house while they are on vacation, sick, or in jail. It's a perfect time to have all your friends over and party a bit. These opportunities are usually advertised in the classifieds, but you may have to ask around to find one.

A Simple Solution

Just stop paying your landlord. See what happens. I have heard of landlords not taking any action against the tenant for *six months!* If you can find any two landlords who are like this, your annual rent would be zero.

These are some methods of not paying rents and living to tell about it. I'm sure that now that you are thinking about it, your devious mind will come up with a few more tricks. Good luck. Only in the good old United States is it possible to live rent free. God bless America!

9. RISING FROM THE DEAD ...

About 2,000 years ago there was this tenant who had a problem with a guy called Pontius Pilate. Pilate thought he got the best of him, but three days later this tenant moved the rock away from his door and rose from the dead. Quite a remarkable feat, but I'm going to tell you how you can do just about the same thing.

Let's say you just stiffed your third landlord in the past six months for the rent. You are going to court and

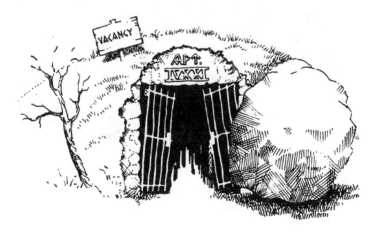

the landlord will probably get a judgment against you for the rent, plus court expenses. This judgment will be recorded and any landlord who belongs to the local credit bureau will have your credit history in five minutes. Let's face it—you are financially dead!

How can you come back from the dead? Take a pencil and paper, hop in the jalopy and head for the cemetery. What you are looking for is a headstone with a name similar to yours, preferably with the same last name. Possibly a deceased member of your family will do. If you can't find any with a similar last name, be sure that at least the first name is the same. That way after you have risen from the dead and you meet an old acquaintance who calls you by your real name (John, Joe, or Bob), it will not cause much concern to whomever you are with.

The next most important thing is age. Check birth dates to get one close to yours. A few years will not matter, but for this ploy to work, you should look the part. Most landlords will question your age and identity if your birth date is 1841.

If you are young, the tombstone pickings may not be too good. I suggest then that you look for the un-natural deaths (war and crime) which usually take people earlier in life. Your cemetery may have a section set aside for the military. That is an excellent place to find young dead. If it does not, then a visit to the local VFW or American Legion is in order. They usually have records of deceased and grave locations for placing flags on Memorial Day. This will make it easy. I would not, under any circumstances, pick any famous person's name.

The graveyard expedition will take a few hours, so take a long some refreshments and possibly a flashlight.

Be sure that the date of birth is within reason and the name is similar (John McGee, J. McKay, Jack MacGee, John McGhey, J. McGay, etc.)

Use caution as you search for a suitable name to resurrect. I heard of a gentleman who was so intent on reading names and dates that he walked into an open grave. This could be embarrassing, especially if they fill it in before you get out.

Now that you have a name and date, proceed to your local registrar of vital statistics and obtain a duplicate birth certificate for the deceased. After you have obtained this, you will be able to obtain a social security card and other documents necessary for renting an apartment without revealing to your potential landlord any past rent problems under your old name.

Obviously the documents are to be used to impress the landlord only. I would not recommend using them to obtain a bank loan, establish credit, obtain a new driver's license because yours was revoked for drunk driving, or seek employment because your work history was erratic.

This is not a foolproof system and I would advise checking the name you pick through the credit bureau before proceeding too far. The person you are selecting for immortality may have had a credit history *worse* than yours! I heard of one case where the name selected and used had an old outstanding warrant for attempted murder! It is wise to check your new identity thoroughly.

Only in the good old United States of America is it possible to come back from the dead. You live in a great country. God bless America!

10. SETTLING THE SCORE

The Bible says, "an eye for an eye, a tooth for a tooth." There is always a chance that one landlord in a million will not be quite perfect. Should you encounter that one in a million case and your landlord takes action against you which disturbs you, you may decide to retaliate.

A simple way to get even is to punch the errant landlord in the face. This is definitely simple, but your risk of trading this landlord for a new one with a star on his vest is great. The new landlord's accommodations may even be less desirable than the present one's. I don't recommend the fist-in-the-face approach, but if you do it, be sure there are no witnesses and you are bigger than the landlord.

As a landlord, I have been on the wrong end of a fist and found it temporarily unpleasant, but I was glad they punched me instead of punching the doors, windows, and walls of my rental unit. I heal automatically and usually for free. Doors, windows, and walls heal only with the assistance of tradesmen, material, and money. The moral of the story is *do something that is going to hurt the landlord in the pocketbook.* The pocketbook is the most painful, vulnerable spot on the landlord's body.

The Ready Mix Concrete Caper

A tenant of mine did not see eye to eye with me on several issues. By mutual agreement, he agreed to vacate, leaving the apartment spotless and in good condition, and I would return his security deposit. On the appointed day and hour, I arrived and checked every possible item I could looking for an excuse to deprive this scum of his security deposit. Everything looked in apple-pie order. I reluctantly gave him his deposit, and he surrendered his keys.

I bet you are thinking, "All's well that ends well." Hardly! The new tenant moved in and immediately

called me to say that none of the drains were working, and that the toilet just overflowed and was dripping through the ceiling downstairs. The downstairs tenant was also a little bit unhappy.

I went over with the plumber and discovered that the main drain in the basement was perfectly okay. The trouble was with the traps on the toilet, bathroom sink, tub, and kitchen sink. They were all filled with hardened concrete. The tenant who moved had purchased a ten-pound bag of Redi-Mix concrete and poured just enough in each drain to fill the trap and let it harden.

The pain in my pocketbook was nearly fatal. I never did locate the ex-tenant to talk to him about his trick, but now I run water in all fixtures before returning the security deposit.

It worked for my tenant and it may work for you.

Let There Be Light

Another technique that will drive a landlord nuts is to play with the electricity. Turn off the electricity. Remove a cover on a wall outlet (one screw in the middle), remove the outlet (two screws—top and bottom). On one side will be a white wire, on the other side a black. Take the white wire and move it over to the same side as the black. This will create a dead short and blow the breaker or fuse as soon as the power is turned back on. To really cause baldness in your landlord, do this to two or three outlets or a ceiling light before you move out. Unless the electrician who tries to resolve this is Thomas Edison himself, it's going to take a few hours to unscramble. It's fairly safe, since a direct short will cut the power, and there is little damage possible if the power goes off. Since the landlord will be inspecting an apartment when no lights or appliances are on, he will probably not notice the lack of power, and you will get your security deposit.

Open Sesame

As you are leaving a residence where the landlord did not appreciate your occupancy, take all the hinge screws out of the front door, except one on each side. The door will open and close enough times for you to get your security deposit back, then fall over as the landlord is showing the apartment to a prospective tenant.

Tenant Organizations

Probably the closest thing to a military coup that occurs in our country is a tenants' organization. They have, in many cases, taken control of the operation of large complexes. It is a good case of the inmates running the asylum. If you really hate your landlord, about the best form of revenge I can think of is to organize all the tenants in the building into a group. In unity there is power. Just look at the progress that the civil rights groups have made in the past few years. If you are successful in starting an organization of this type, you may be able to:

• Withhold rent until repairs or improvements are made

• Obtain fast response from building and health departments

• Retain an attorney to represent members in their grievances with the landlord

• Numerous other things that an individual would not be able to accomplish.

Landlords dread this type of alliance. It is not a fair fight with its 150 tenants against one landlord. Even the ratio of Christians to lions was better.

A tenant's organization is always able to attract attention from the media. The media's sympathy is with the underdog. Although the landlord is usually right and the tenant wrong, the media will be biased and portray the landlord as the villain.

If the landlord gives you a hard time, organize, elect officers, schedule meetings, and make ridiculous demands like a 10 percent rent decrease. Start your own revolution. If you are successful, you will get revenge and better living conditions. If you are not successful, you may find two big guys with tattoos and leather jackets moving your earthly possessions out in the street.

More Techniques

Most of these techniques are for use when you want

to create a problem after you have left and received
your security. Be sure the landlord gives you cash—not
a check—or he may stop payment after the problems are
discovered. Tell him you need cash because you are leaving the area or country and won't have a bank account
for some time.

If you don't care about your security deposit, want
to torment your landlord without mercy, dream of
becoming a one-man army of devastation and driving
this wayward landlord to the insane asylum, I recommend *Get Even, Up Yours!,* and *The Revenge Book,* all
available through Paladin Press. These books are available for entertainment purposes only but they certainly
will stimulate your creativity.

You will have peace of mind by getting the last
laugh on your landlord, some tradesmen will get a few
hours of work, the landlord will put some of his money
back into circulation to stimulate our sagging economy,
and America will be stronger for your efforts. You are
a patriotic American. God bless America!

11. VARMINTS AND VERMIN

Depending on what area of the country you live in, you may inherit co-tenants in your humble dwelling. Unless you are fond of roaches, rats, lizards, worms, bats, lice, and creepy crawlers of all colors, you may not want these little friends sharing your space and eating

your groceries before you do. They are very hard to get rid of.

A parallel has been drawn between the cockroach and the dinosaur. They are both from about the same period of time. People have always tried to eliminate the cockroach. In the old days, they whacked it with a rock. Modern sprays are used today and still the roaches are with us. No one ever tried to eradicate the dinosaur, but he is gone today. The roaches are still around. If they are hardy enough to outlast the gigantic dinosaur, I don't think we will ever wipe them out. We may succeed in stopping them for a week or two, but they will be back.

I once had a building nearly destroyed by fire. It was in the dead of winter, and temperatures were below zero. The building was first subjected to extreme heat. Metal beams melted. Then the building was left to the elements for about thirty days. When we began restoration, the roaches were still in the walls.

If you are inspecting an apartment, one of the first things you should look for are the little creatures. They won't be standing in the middle of the room where you can see them. They will be hiding under the sink, in the cupboards, in the bathroom medicine cabinet, and in closets. Look for them before you decide to rent. I'm not sure you will ever find an apartment without roaches, but there's always that chance.

Maybe you purchased this book after you already moved into a roach-infested palace. There is still hope. These little pests are against the law. The health department frowns on their existence in buildings, and your landlord is responsible for exterminating them. Before you bother him, try some roach spray or rat poison. If the problem is small enough, you may be able to take care of it yourself. Your landlord is not going to be happy if you ask him to call the exterminators.

Most landlords feel that the infestation problem is caused by the tenants and their poor housekeeping. They do not feel that they should be forced to correct a problem that was caused by tenants. The landlord is liable for the extermination, however, so you can press it. If he refuses to handle the problem, call the health department. Show the inspector the dead rat, lizard, or roach. If you can't find one, borrow one from your neighbor. Ask the inspector for his name and his superior's name. If he thinks you may turn him in if he doesn't do his job, he will be on his toes. In some areas, the health department will actually contact the exterminator and bill the landlord.

I once heard of a tenant who became upset over the varmint problem in his complex. He obtained a sampling of the various sized roaches, about a hundred or so live healthy ones, and placed them in a large envelope with his rent check. He carefully sealed the corners with tape and mailed the envelope to his landlord. The landlord tore open the envelope in his living room and was greatly surprised by the army of creatures that scattered throughout his lovely home. I don't recommend sending live creatures through the mail, but it worked for this tenant. The landlord immediately contacted an exterminator and had the tenant's apartment and his own home sprayed.

If you are successful in ridding your residence of unasked for pets, a good way to keep it that way is by proper housekeeping. When you're finished that greasy pizza, throw the remnants and the box out the window. Don't leave it around overnight. Keep food in tightly capped containers; wipe up any spills immediately. It's just common sense to keep your living area clean, but my experiences indicate that the level of common sense in tenants is not at the high level it is in a landlord. Give it a try, and you may help keep our country free of varmints and vermin. God bless America!

12. EQUAL HOUSING

Very simply put, no landlord may refuse to rent to you because of your race, color, religion, sex, or national origin. Equal opportunity in housing is the law in the U.S.A.

The Civil Rights Act of 1866 provides that "all citizens of the United States shall have the same right, in every state and territory, as is enjoyed by white citizens thereof to inherit, purchase, lease, sell, hold, and convey real and personal property." Title VIII of the 1968 Rights Act is known as the Federal Fair Housing Law. The law makes illegal any discrimination in the sale, lease, or rental of real property based on race, color, religion, sex, or national origin. Everyone should receive the same treatment and be able to obtain the same accommodations.

Landlords and the Law

I have found that by and large landlords comply with these laws. It's not that they want to rent to minorities, it's just that they don't want to spend time in court defending their case of why they denied someone a rental. Time is money. If you take your attorney with you to court, time will be a *lot* of money. These cases are usually decided in a court with a jury made up of tenants. Any self-respecting landlord finds a way to avoid jury duty, so the jury pool is usually 95 percent tenants. You will probably be the winner against the landlord, and he knows that. So if he denies you an apartment and you are a girl, indicate that you noticed he favors guys in renting. Wave an Equal Housing pamphlet around, and I think he will decide that you fit in after all. The pamphlets are available through the Department of Housing and Urban Development (HUD) or through your local real estate board. Complaints alleging discrimination may be filed with the nearest HUD office.

Easy Money

Are you down and out? Is there only dog food left in your cupboard and you don't have a dog? Did the bank just repossess your car with your girl friend sleeping in the back seat? I can tell you a pretty sure-fire way to get discriminated against.

Pack a bag, take a tape recorder and a friend as a

witness, go to Chinatown (if you are Chinese, go to the local "Little Italy"), and find a nice-looking apartment house with a vacancy sign.

You will undoubtedly get a very cold welcome since ethnic groups like to rent to their kind to keep peace and harmony. Usually you will be turned away. Be sure you talk directly to the landlord and document his name, time, date, response, and your witness's name. Find a young, ball-of-fire, just-out-of-law-school attorney, and stake your claim. This is called a nuisance suit. Before long the landlord will offer you a settlement to avoid going to court. Consider this fast, easy money and decide what you can do with it. Is it enough to convert the dogfood in the cupboard to filet mignon, or should you go to court to get more? Give it a try. You are actually helping America keep its landlords honest while picking up some pocket change to survive on. That's the American way. God bless America!

13. NO REPAIRS AND REPAIRS

Many times landlords are reluctant to make repairs. This is especially true when the cause of the damage is the tenant. If your ex-husband kicked in the front door and knocked a hole in the wall with your head, the landlord will not be overjoyed at spending his money to repair your damage. On the other hand, the normal repairs necessary to maintain the property in good condition are the responsibility of the landlord.

Your landlord is out to make a buck and will probably not make repairs immediately after your request. It may take some effort to get his attention which may be disturbing if you must live with the problem. Give your landlord every opportunity to make repairs, and if that fails, you may decide on another path to getting what you want.

Government Agencies

If the disrepair affects your health or safety—such as electrical, plumbing, heating, stairs, or fire exits— building or health codes are probably being violated and the appropriate agency should be contacted. They will send out an inspector to verify that the problem exists and then either correct the problem, or demand that the landlord correct the problem by a specific date.

Be sure that when the inspector arrives the problem is evident. If it is a periodic problem, you may wish to recreate it before he visits. For example, say that the toilet does not always flush. Stuff half a loaf of bread in it before the inspector arrives. After he leaves, you can plunge the bread out and continue using the toilet until repairs are complete. By recreating the problem, you will enable the inspector to tell his supervisor about it, and they will order the landlord to have it permanently fixed.

Playing on the Landlord's Sympathy

This may or may not work. A lot depends on your landlord. He may be a push-over, and then again, he may not be. It won't hurt to give it a try. Mention the danger bare wires pose to you or your kids, the incon-

venience of throwing your bathwater out the window because the drain doesn't work, etc., and many landlords will take care of the problem just to shut you up. If your landlord is employed, call his office at noon while he is at lunch. Give your hard luck story to his secretary. Embellish it—"We have been without hot water for two weeks," or "The baby is turning blue from the cold." Getting the message from a co-worker may shame him into action.

If you have a talented friend, have him call the landlord's office and say, "This is Father McGuire from St. Francis Parish. One of our parishioners, the widow Mrs. Joe Tenant, is being inconvenienced by the rats running amuck in her apartment. I am sure Mr. Landlord would have the good Lord's blessing, if he were to eliminate this dreadful condition." The power of the cloth sometimes *does* work miracles.

The Self-Help Method

Use this as a last resort only! My tenants have pulled this off with amazing results. Call a tradesman in the Yellow Pages (plumber, electrician, heating contractor, etc.), and tell him that you, J.P. Landlord, owner of 501 Scum Street, would like to have the drain unplugged at that property. Give your landlord's address for the bill. The handyman will probably come out and fix your drain, and your problem will be solved. The landlord will not know which tenant in the building used this approach, but he will be stuck with the bill.

If the problem is common only to your apartment, you have to be a little more evasive. Your faucet is running full blast, the drain is plugged, and it takes all your time bailing out the sink. The landlord has not sent a plumber. If you call and have one sent to your apartment, your landlord will know who to kill. So, first check with some of the other tenants to see if they have any plumbing problems. If they do, make a list, call the plumber, and say you are J.P. Landlord and would like him to fix the faucet in 3-A, the tub in 2-C, and the toilet in 10-B. Have the bill sent to the landlord's address.

If your landlord is a real stiff, you may have to call several tradesmen before you find one who will work for him without seeing the green of his money first. Keep trying. The Yellow Pages are thick, and there is bound to be one who will take the bait.

No one is going to lose. You get your repairs, the tradesman will give the bill to his attorney if the landlord does not pay, and the attorney will collect through the courts. Since the landlord will seem like a dead beat (the work was done to his property at "his" request), the courts will make him pay. That is certainly justice! That is what our country is all about. God bless America!

14. EVICTION

This word strikes fear in the hearts of most tenants. Cancer, VD, and botulism are minor problems when compared to eviction. The eviction is the last straw for both the landlord and the tenant. All else has failed, the sentence has been given by the court: *move, or we will move you!*

No landlord is happy to go through an eviction. It costs much time and money and usually a tenant being

tossed out will do additional damage on his way. So I offer a few words to the wise which may make moving a little less traumatic.

Partial Payment

Let's say you are three months behind in your rent, and you have just received a final notice from the landlord saying that he is going to take you to court. He doesn't really want to, so if you offer him partial payment, he may get off your case for a few more weeks. Tell him you have one month's rent and will have the balance in three weeks. Most landlords will take what they can get and hope you will come through as agreed with the balance. Half a loaf is better than none. If your landlord does take you to court, he will have to pay the attorney, the process server, the movers, and the company that stores your junk. If you have some dough and he takes your offer, you will buy some time.

If You Are Broke

If you plain and simple do not have any money and that is the reason you did not pay the past few months' rent, here is a good way to finance your move. When the landlord presents his final demand to you to get out or go to court, tell him you will move *if he gives you $150 cash*. It's not as crazy as it sounds. If the landlord goes to court, his expenses will exceed your modest demand, he will have to spend the time required to appear in court, and you will be occupying the apartment for another month or so without paying rent.

Many times I have succumbed to the tenant's demand for cash to get out. I have even suggested the cash bonus many times to eliminate the time and efforts required for eviction.

The Stall

In some areas it takes six or seven weeks to get an eviction case on the docket. If you are stalling for time, wait until your case is ready to come up, then call the landlord. Tell him you have $100 and will have the balance next week. If he takes the money and allows you to stay, he may have to start the proceeding all over again, and you will buy six more weeks time for your $100.

Illegal Evictions

The eviction must be court ordered to be legal. If the landlord arrives with a goon squad and starts relocating your possessions to the curb, you can get help.

If your landlord is evicting you illegally, call the police and have him arrested. Or sue him for damages. If you do not have an attorney, try a legal clinic which operates at reduced fees. If you are on welfare or assistance, the legal aid attorneys will handle your complaint.

If your landlord attempts to throw you and your brats out using force, consider using force yourself. Do you have any big friends? Invite them over when you expect the landlord to visit. A man's home is his castle and even though you are only renting your castle, you do have some rights.

Constructive Eviction

This is a legal term that means something has been done to the property to prevent you from peacefully occupying the premises. Maybe the landlord is trying to get you out so he can convert to condominiums or remodel and rerent at a higher rent. Or maybe he doesn't want to spend the time and money on a long, drawn-out

On any winter day, housing officials estimate that thousands of New Yorkers are without heat and hot water. They live in slum neighborhoods in buildings that landlords have milked and abandoned. They live in up-and-coming communities, such as Boerum Hill, where "gentrification" is driving up housing costs and driving out the poor. And they appear even in the city's more affluent sections.

A record number of calls are flooding the city's central complaint number—11,618 on Jan. 11 alone, the day the temperature plummeted to 5 degrees. City housing lawyers expect to sue the owners of as many as 5,000 buildings this year to try to force them to provide heat—well above the record 3,000 suits filed last year.

● Kenneth Noonan, a 6-foot-3, 250-pounder, who, according to one of his tenants, threatened he would "break my head" for organizing tenants to demand heat and hot water.

● Jacob Finkelstein, who was fined $20,000 this month for turning off the heat and hot water in two Manhattan buildings—and whose own Brooklyn home is to be picketed today by 50 angry tenants.

Then there's Waldro Gooden, the landlord wh stopped heating his building at 2328 Bedford Ave., Brooklyn, and then told a housing court judge he wouldn't turn the heat back on. That was the event that made him the only landlord jailed this winter.

Or Max Silverberg, a 70-year-old widower. His living room walls glisten with icicles. His kitchen floor is sheathed in ice half an inch thick. And a six-by-four-foot hole gapes above his kitchen table—caused by a pipe that froze, burst and deluged his ceiling with so much water the plaster collapsed.

ourt eviction, so he disables the heating system and says he is unable to locate the parts to fix it. He may turn off the electricity or water for a long period of time or take out the windows in winter.

All these tactics are illegal but they are frequently used to rid a building of the occupants. If your landlord does any of these, immediately notify the building bureau and the health department. Many times they are able to have the heat or electricity restored immediately and bill the landlord. After you call, have *every* tenant call. The number of complaints will speed the response of the proper authorities. As the previous clippings indicate, the constructive eviction practice is common in many cities and can result in fines or jail for the landlord.

The laws are on your side as a tenant. Our country has always bent over backward to protect the underdogs (tenants). Don't be afraid to contact the authorities with your complaint. You will be heard, and if you are not, call the media. They love tenant/landlord problems and will jump at the chance to photograph your freezing kids for the evening news.

15. BE YOUR OWN LANDLORD

Did you ever hear the song "I'm my own grandpa?" It was a complicated song about how someone married his cousin's mother's sister, had children, and then through assorted family connections, finally became his own grandfather. Becoming your own landlord is much easier.

I once owned a five-family dwelling. One tenant in this building had been there eight years when I purchased it. He stayed during my entire ownership, and his rent was exactly the amount of the mortgage. The tenant actually bought the building for me! He stayed after I sold it, but I stopped by last year out of curiosity to see if he was still there. He wasn't, but the young man who answered the door knew me. How could this be? I didn't know him. He explained that when I last saw him he was younger and smaller. He was the past tenant's son. His mother and father had retired after thirty years from their important jobs of packing film in yellow boxes. They had moved down South, and the son had taken over the apartment. Their total time in residence was twenty-six years! The son had been there four more for a family total of thirty years. They had actually paid in rent two-and-a-half times what I paid for the building, yet they didn't own even a single door-knob for all that money!

Some tenants just do not want to become property owners because they do not like responsibility. If you fit that pattern, skip this chapter or you will be wasting your time. That time could be better spent beating your fat wife or going bowling with the guys you work with on the trash truck. But if you are interested in raising your status from a lowly tenant to the high-class land-lord, read on.

Some Methods of Becoming Your Own Landlord

One of the advantages of being a landlord is the tax break. The government allows the landlord to deduct a certain amount each year for depreciation. When those years have passed, the depreciation is no longer allowed, and the landlord's tax is much higher. At this time he may very well consider liquidating the property. You could actually become the proud owner of your slum. You would not have to move, change your phone number, or notify your parole officer. You could throw out the little old lady upstairs with the stinking tomcat and replace her with a topless dancer.

If the landlord is willing to sell, the best way for you to proceed is for him to "hold the mortgage." This will be to his advantage because he will continue to receive income from the property yet not have the problems and headaches associated with dealing with the tenants. If he is willing to sell the property to you, you will make a down payment, the amount of which is nego-tiable between you and the landlord. Your attorney will draw up all the papers necessary for transferring the title to you. You will then collect all the rents, pay the ex-landlord a set amount, and retain the balance for fun and games. Every month you will be reducing the amount you owe which is known as *building equity*. Eventually the payments to the ex-landlord will stop and the property will be yours! All the interest, taxes, and upkeep expenses are deductible so your income taxes will be reduced considerably. Nice country we live in!

Some Other Ways

Maybe the building you live in is not for sale. Then I suggest consulting a realtor. If you have a large down payment, a good job, and good credit, most realtors will welcome you with open arms. The problem arises when you are less than affluent, your only income is picking up scrap with a shopping cart, and your credit history resembles Jessie Jame's list of train robberies. You may have to look a little harder then to find a broker willing to assist you in becoming a landlord. Rest assured, though, regardless of your financial position, there is a realtor out there who can be of assistance. You will have to hunt for him. Ask friends who have purchased property who their realtor was. Watch the classifieds for handyman specials or distress sales. Find out which brokers handle these deals. Many times clients come into our real estate office after being ignored by other offices because of their financial condition. We have found properties for them. I have taken motorcycles, boats, trailers, furniture, cameras, and guns as down payment on properties. Forget using your old lady as a down payment. There are too many available to make them worth anything.

Beat the Condo Conversion

Maybe the property you reside in is slated for conversion to condos. If the building is small enough and your fellow tenants are willing, there is a chance your landlord will sell the property to you as a group for a small profit rather than spend the time and money renovating and marketing the units. If you and the other tenants owned your own slum, you could do anything you wanted without fear of being evicted (raise goats on the roof, rent only to hookers, etc.). If you decide to buy the joint in conjunction with the other tenants, be sure to include an attorney in the group to give you legal representation and draw up the papers necessary for acquisition. Many times it actually costs less to own and manage the property than it did to rent. You also receive all the tax breaks that a homeowner receives.

16. TIPS, TALES, AND TRIVIA

Being at the intellectual level they are, most tenants aren't able to think up the suggestions listed in this chapter. But as a landlord, I've seen most all the tricks—from the best to the worst. And with my naturally analytical landlord's mind, I've carefully worked at perfecting my methods for neutralizing most of the shenanigans my tenants pull.

I'm going to share a few of them with you here. Lord only knows I've been good (I'm writing this book for tenants, aren't I?) and I don't deserve any of you readers as future renters.

The Classifieds

In many newspapers, classified ads are categorized by the item (apartment, car, etc.) then alphabetized by address (AAB Street to Zegment Drive). In my opinion, tenants are creatures of habit. They will go directly to the classification they desire (furnished apartment) and call the ad at the head of the column. The landlord with an apartment on AAB Street will get dozens of calls and many tenants to choose from. Tenants going to see that apartment will be competing with many others. They may miss a ball game on TV, or their beers may go flat while they are out looking at this hovel.

Here is a secret known only to me, and now, you. Start at the bottom! Call the apartment on Zegment Street. That landlord will probably not get any calls except yours. Go over and see the shack. Tell him the rent is too high. Since you are the only one who called or looked at it, he may believe you and drop it ten bucks.

Too Hot or Too Cold?

Is the thermostat in your apartment building in a pretty little plastic box? Only the landlord has the key to it, only the landlord can set it up or down—that's what you think! This plastic box is a pacifier for the landlord. Any tenant over the age of three can circumvent this locked thermostat. If your apartment is cold, pack this plastic box with snow, or hang a plastic bag filled with ice cubes over the box. If it controls the air conditioner and you are too hot, aim a hair dryer at the plastic box, or put a light bulb under it.

These boxes all have air slots so the thermostat will sense the temperature. A coat hanger will go through the same slot and you can turn the thermostat up or down. If the thermostat is completely inaccessible, but you can find the wire that goes to it, you can cut across the two low-voltage wires with a razor blade which will cause the furnace or air conditioner to activate.

More Light

Many hall lights are controlled by a photo cell placed to sense the exterior, natural light. When the sun shines into the sensor, the inside lights are switched off. When it gets dark, they are switched on. Your job is to make the sensor think it is dark all the time. Locate the sensor. It's usually in a small box with a tiny window facing east to catch the morning sun. Place tape over this window and your lights are on all the time.

Half Off Your Phone Bill

This discount is not actually offered by the phone company, so don't contact them. Instead contact your next-door neighbor (or downstairs or upstairs neighbor). Tell him you will pay half of his phone bill if you can run a wire from his phone to your apartment. You can buy or borrow a phone, and the wire is readily available at any hardware store. Connecting it is simple if you have a plug-in module and slightly harder if you have a hardwired set. If your area phones are hardwired, just match up the colors (red to red, green to green, etc.)

Free Magazines

Find out the name of the previous tenant. Get a subscription order card for your favorite girlie magazine. You can rip one out of the magazine at the newsstand and subscribe to it in his name. Send no money. They will bill the previous tenant. The magazine will arrive because when people change their addresses, they usually mark the box that says they will not pay forwarding postage for the books and magazines. The books will come to your address and the bill will be forwarded to the previous tenant. Enjoy yourself.

Save Electricity

Usually the electric panel boxes for each apartment are located in the basement. Yours may have three or four separate circuits. Have a friend who is an electrician move one or two of these to the panel box for an adjoining apartment or to the box for the hall lights. It's a simple job and will take him only about ten minutes. The savings to you will be substantial and the other tenants will probably think the electric company raised the rates.

Valuables

Most of my tenants do not have many items of value—probably just a couple of baseball cards and a matchbook with a nude chick on the back. You, being a much higher caliber tenant (you bought this book, didn't you?), may have more precious items (a Timex watch, silver dollar, etc.). Apartments are often robbed. You are living in a den of thieves. Most will think of looking in your freezer, under your mattress, and in the cookie jar, even though the cookie jar is protected by an army of attack cockroaches.

Take out your largest bureau drawer. Put it on the bed and staple or tape a large, heavy-weight envelope to the back of the drawer. Most burglars will open the drawer and throw the things in it on the floor but not actually remove the drawer to find your hidden envelope. You may also throw a burglar off the track with a decoy. Take an old billfold. Put some small money in it, expired credit cards, and a photo of your three illegitimate kids. "Hide" it in the top drawer of the bureau. When a hopped-up junkie breaks in to steal something to sell so he can get his daily fix, he will grab your decoy and run.

Free Medical Care

If you happen to be a sky diver, bouncer at a bar, stock car driver, stunt man, semipro hockey player, or have some other type of dangerous hobby, you may from time to time receive some disabling injuries. In the past you probably went directly to the hospital and had your bones set. You also lost time from your crummy job (if you have one) and had to pay the doctor out of your own cash.

The next time you slide into third base and break your ankle, don't go directly to the hospital. Instead, have someone take you home. Remove the bulb from the rear hall light and then pound on the stairs, yell and lay down at the foot of the stairs. When the other tenants come running to see what happened, explain that you fell down the stairs in the dark and broke your ankle. Have the tenants call an ambulance and the police so a report is made. Be sure the officer notices the missing bulb and the dark hall. You get a nice ambulance ride and good attention at the hospital, since they know you are insured, and they will be paid.

Get a copy of the police report and call the land-lord's insurance company. If he is reluctant to give you the name of his company, contact a lawyer and begin suit against the landlord. He will immediately get his in-surance company on the case to prevent any personal financial loss. Your settlement will be substantial and include medical bills, loss of earnings, and an amount for pain and suffering. If your fat old lady is still living with you, she may even get something for loss of your services!

I once had a tenant who was a hooker and sus-tained a fractured foot in an "on the job accident"— something about getting her foot caught under the dash-board of a sports car. She insisted that she slipped on the ice on my building's steps. She nearly received a settlement from my insurance company, but another tenant who lived in the building told the court that he saw her get out of the car limping before the alleged slip on my step.

It works most of the time. Give it a try. The insur-ance company won't miss a few bucks and you can probably catch up on some of your back rent. People sue all the time. It's the American way. God bless America!

17. AND THEY LIVED HAPPILY...

Not quite, but it sounds good. This country would definitely be a better place, if by some chance, tenants and landlords could live together in harmony. It's definitely wishful thinking, but it would certainly make my job as a landlord more pleasant and less work. I imagine that landlords and tenants will probably see eye-to-eye about the same time the U.S. and the USSR become kissing cousins.

Believe it or not, your landlord is not out to get you. He just wants the rent you agreed to pay when you moved in. He wants you to take care of his property. He wants you to return his call when you have problems paying. He wants you to come to the door when he knocks. He does not want to do physical or mental battle with you, unless absolutely necessary. He wants to get along with you.

If you cooperate with the landlord, you will have peace of mind and possibly better living conditions. If you are openly hostile with your landlord and he comes to the end of his rope with you, you'll be wise to start looking for an apartment with an immediate vacancy. Remember, it's easier to move than spend time recuperating from landlord-inflicted injuries, or do time for landlord abuse. This is a good country we live in. Americans can move anywhere any time they want to. God bless America!